THE TECHNIQUE OF ORCHESTRATION WORKBOOK

The Technique of Orchestration Workbook, Seventh Edition, accompanies the textbook of the same name—the definitive resource on the study of orchestration—providing musical excerpts, full scores, and scoring assignments to enrich the lessons learned in the textbook. Spanning an array of periods and styles, the musical examples collected here cover scoring techniques in the following sections:

- Strings
- Woodwinds
- Brass
- Scoring of Chords
- Transcribing Piano Music
- Scoring for Woodwinds, Horns, and Strings
- Percussion
- Harp and Keyboard Instruments
- Scoring for Full Orchestra

Additional learning tools include transposition exercises, error detection drills, and discussions on harmonics, while the workbook pages are perforated throughout for ease of use in and out of the classroom. Featuring the music of Bach, Mozart, Brahms, Beethoven, Schumann, Copland, Bartók, and many more, *The Technique of Orchestration Workbook*, Seventh Edition, is an invaluable companion to the textbook.

Kent Kennan (1913–2003) was an American composer and Professor Emeritus of Music at the University of Texas at Austin.

Donald Grantham is an award-winning composer and the Frank C. Erwin, Jr. Centennial Professor of Music at the University of Texas at Austin.

THE TECHNIQUE OF ORCHESTRATION WORKBOOK

Seventh Edition

Kent Kennan

The University of Texas at Austin

Donald Grantham

The University of Texas at Austin

Routledge
Taylor & Francis Group
NEW YORK AND LONDON

Cover image: furtseff/Shutterstock.com

Seventh edition published 2024
by Routledge
605 Third Avenue, New York, NY 10158

and by Routledge
4 Park Square, Milton Park, Abingdon, Oxon, OX14 4RN

Routledge is an imprint of the Taylor & Francis Group, an informa business

© 2024 Donald Grantham

The right of Kent Kennan and Donald Grantham to be identified as authors of this work has been asserted in accordance with sections 77 and 78 of the Copyright, Designs and Patents Act 1988.

All rights reserved. No part of this book may be reprinted or reproduced or utilised in any form or by any electronic, mechanical, or other means, now known or hereafter invented, including photocopying and recording, or in any information storage or retrieval system, without permission in writing from the publishers.

Trademark notice: Product or corporate names may be trademarks or registered trademarks, and are used only for identification and explanation without intent to infringe.

First edition published by Prentice Hall 1952

Sixth edition published by Prentice Hall 2002

ISBN: 978-0-367-67297-3 (hbk)
ISBN: 978-0-367-65560-0 (pbk)
ISBN: 978-1-003-13069-7 (ebk)

DOI: 10.4324/9781003130697

Typeset in Baskerville
by Deanta Global Publishing Services, Chennai, India

CONTENTS

In cases where a piece of music lends itself to scoring for orchestral groups other than the one under which it is listed here, the alternative possibilities are indicated by means of letters:

W	woodwinds
B	brass
S	strings
WHS	woodwinds, horns, and strings
O	orchestra

Thus, (S, O) after a title listed under woodwinds means that the music is also suitable for an assignment in scoring for strings or for orchestra.

An asterisk (*) indicates the complete work is provided.

STRINGS (CHAPTERS 3, 4)   1

    J. S. Bach (harmonization), **Was Frag Ich Nach Der Welt** (W, B, WHS, O)   1
    Crusaders' Hymn (W, B WHS, O)   1
    J. S. Bach (harmonization), **Aus Tiefer Not** (W, B, WHS, O)   1
    J. S. Bach, **Sarabande*** from the First French Suite   2
    Exercises in Bowing; Use of Alto and Tenor Clefs (selected fragments)   3
    Exercises in Bowing; Use of Alto and Tenor Clefs (selected fragments)   5
    Mozart, **Sonata in B-Flat Major**, third movement (WHS)   7
    Exercise in Error Detection (strings) based on **Träumerei** from **Scenes from Childhood**   9
    Brahms, **Romanze**, Op. 118, No. 5   10
    Beethoven, **Sonata**, Op. 10, No. 3   11
    Schumann, **Papillons**, No. 5   11
    Mennin, **Aria**, from **Five Piano Pieces**   12
    Exercises in Writing Multiple Stops   13
    Beethoven, **Sonata**, Op. 13 (for writing multiple stops)   13
    Exercises in Reading and Notating String Harmonics   14
    Vaughan Williams, **Fantasia on "Greensleeves,"** score study   15

WOODWINDS (CHAPTERS 5, 6)   27

    Exercises in Notating Transposing Woodwinds (selected fragments)   27
    Exercise in Error Detection (woodwinds) based on Haydn **Sonata in D**   29
    Schubert, **Sonata**, Op. 122, first movement (S, WHS)   30
    Kuhlau, **Sonatina**, Op. 55, No. 4, second movement*   31
    Beethoven, **Sonata**, Op. 2, No. 3, third movement (S, WHS)   33

Bartók, No. 21* from **Little Pieces for Children**, Vol. 1 (S, WHS) — 34
J. S. Bach (harmonization), **Christus, Der Ist Mein Leben** (B, WHS, O) — 35
Hindemith, **Fuga Secunda in G** from **Ludus Tonalis** (S, WHS, O) — 36
Bartók, **Concerto for Orchestra**, second movement, score study — 37

BRASS (CHAPTERS 7, 8, 9) — 48
Conversion of Parts for Horns and Trumpets in Various Keys to Concert Pitches — 48
J. S. Bach (harmonization), **O Haupt Voll Blut Und Wunden** (W, S, WHS, O) — 50
America (S, WHS, O) — 51
Morley, **Damon and Phillis** from **Canzonets or Little Short Airs to Five and Six Voices** — 52
Grieg, **Sailor's Song*** — 53
Schumann, **War Song** from **Album for the Young** — 54
Mussorgsky, **Promenade** from **Pictures from an Exhibition** — 54
Bartók, **Folk Song**, No. 8* from **Ten Easy Pieces** for piano (WHS, O) — 55

SCORING OF CHORDS (CHAPTER 10) — 56
Chords for Orchestra, score study — 56
For woodwinds in pairs; for full woodwind section; for brass; for strings — 59
For "average" orchestra; for large orchestra — 60
For woodwinds in pairs; for brass; for woodwinds in pairs and two horns — 61
For "average" orchestra; for large orchestra — 62

PROBLEMS IN TRANSCRIBING PIANO MUSIC (CHAPTER 11) — 63
Transcribing Piano Music for Orchestra, score study — 63
Rearrangement of pianistic figures (selected fragments) — 68
Beethoven, **Sonata**, Op. 10, No. 3, first movement — 69
Beethoven, **Sonata**, Op. 22, first movement — 70

SCORING FOR WOODWINDS, HORNS, AND STRINGS (CHAPTER 12) — 71
Scoring for Woodwinds, Horns and Strings, *The Technique of Orchestration*, pp. 216–222, score study — 71
Beethoven, **Sonata**, Op. 90, first movement — 74
Tchaikovsky, **At Church*** from **Album for the Young** — 76
Chopin, **Nocturne**, Op. 55, no 1 (fragment to be scored four ways) — 77
Beethoven, **Sonata**, Op. 27, No. 1, fourth movement — 79
Brahms, **Variations and Fugue on a Theme by Handel**, Var. X — 79
Kabalevsky, **Sonatina**, Op. 13, No. 1 (S, O) — 80

PERCUSSION (CHAPTERS 13, 14) — 81
Schumann, **Important Event*** from **Scenes from Childhood** (timpani part) — 81
Kabalevsky, **Prelude 24** from **24 Preludes** (percussion parts) — 82
Prokofiev, **March** from **The Love of Three Oranges** (percussion parts) — 83

HARP (CHAPTER 15) — 84
Kennan, Harp Exercises (rewriting enharmonically) — 84
Kennan, Harp Exercises (rewriting, setting pedals for glissandos) — 85

CONTENTS

ORCHESTRA (CHAPTER 16) — **87**
    Bartók, No. 12 from **Fifteen Hungarian Peasant Songs** (WHS plus perc.) — 87
    Crusaders' Hymn — 87
    Exercise in Error Detection (orchestra) — 88
    Bartók, No. 1 from **Fifteen Hungarian Peasant Songs** (WHS) — 89
    Schumann, **Fantasia**, Op. 17 — 90
    MacDowell, **A Deserted Farm*** — 91
    Tcherepnine, No. 1 from **Ten Bagatelles**, Op. 5 — 92
    Grieg, **Notturno**, Op. 54, No. 4 (WHS) — 94
    Schubert, **Sonata**, Op. 143, first movement — 96
    Copland, **Heart, We Will Forget Him*** from **Eight Songs of Emily Dickinson** — 97
    Kennan, Exercises in Scoring in the Styles of Debussy and Strauss — 99
    J. S. Bach, **Fugue VII*** from **The Well Tempered Clavier**, Volume II — 100
    Brahms, **Rhapsody**, Op. 79, No. 1 — 102
    Griffes, **The White Peacock** from **Three Roman Sketches** — 104
    Rochberg, **Bagatelle 8*** from **Twelve Bagatelles** — 106
    Prokofiev, **March**, Op. 12, No. 1 — 107

SCORING FOR HIGH SCHOOL ORCHESTRA (CHAPTER 19) — **109**
    Debussy, **Golliwogg's Cake Walk** from **The Children's Corner** — 109

PREFACE

The workbook accompanying *The Technique of Orchestration* has undergone three previous editions. Following each of these editions, the authors queried a number of teachers about which exercises were found to be the most useful for the beginning student. This new edition of the workbook retains all of these proven exercises plus a new kind of exercise not found in previous editions. For the musical examples in *The Technique of Orchestration*, Seventh Edition, chapters dealing with: scoring of chords; problems in transcribing piano music; and scoring for woodwind, horns, and strings; score study questions are provided that are designed to help students learn what to look for as they begin examining orchestral scores. These exercises may be assigned for students to complete independently, or they can be used in class as a guide for discussion.

Also new in this edition is a complete short work for strings, Ralph Vaughan Williams's *Fantasia on "Greensleeves,"* and an excerpt from Bartók's *Concerto for Orchestra* (2nd movement). Each of these works is accompanied by basic score study questions.

The exercises are arranged in an overall sequence that corresponds with the order of presentation in *The Technique of Orchestration*, Seventh Edition, by Kent Kennan and Donald Grantham (Routledge, 2024); they are listed in the Table of Contents, along with references to the particular chapters for which they may best serve as assignments. Some lend themselves to scoring for other orchestral groups as well, and these alternative possibilities are also indicated. There is no intention that any one class should do all the exercises in each section. In the case of the more basic assignments, each type is presented twice, with a different musical basis each time. This plan allows for some variation in material assigned from year to year. As for the other less elementary material, each instructor must of course choose whichever exercises seem best suited to his or her students' needs and abilities. Most of the assignments are aimed at the student in a first-year orchestration course, but some in the last portion of the workbook are of a difficulty that may make them more suitable for an advanced course.

The assignments are arranged in two different formats: (1) the music is given in its original form at the bottom of the page with blank staves above on which the scoring is to be done; (2) the music alone is given, the scoring to be done on a separate sheet. The first arrangement has the advantage of saving the student considerable time that he or she would otherwise spend in setting up the page; the second assures learning the correct placement of instruments on the page and the general mechanics of score writing.

Kent Kennan
Donald Grantham

STRINGS
Chapters 3, 4

Score one of the excerpts below (as specified by the instructor) for strings in six different ways. Use Examples 3.3–3.6 and 3.8–3.11 in Chapter 3 of the text as general models. It is not necessary to rewrite the clef, key signature, meter signature, or tempo indication in versions 2, 3, 5, and 6. In version 6, make plentiful use of octave doublings. No bowing indications need be included. Tempo markings and dynamics in parentheses were added for purposes of this assignment.

STRINGS

Score for strings. Dynamics will have to be added, since none are included in the original; they should reflect the *espressivo* character of the music without producing an over-romantic effect. The F♯ and E♭ half notes in measure 12 and the F♯ quarter note in measure 15 are best moved up an octave for reasons of consistent voice-leading and range of instruments. It is suggested that the instructor discuss the question of octave doublings as it applies here, also that of characteristic Baroque bowing. (Bowing indications should be included.)

SARABANDE

From the First French Suite

J.S. Bach

Exercises in Bowing and in the Use of Alto and Tenor Clefs

Each of the following fragments is given first with the phrasing used in the original (piano) version, and on the staff below without phrasing. To this latter version, add bowing indications (slurs, up-bow and down-bow signs where necessary, etc.). Aim at the general effect of the original. Exercises 5 to 8 also involve writing the melody in the clef shown. In Exercise 9, observe the transposition used by the double bass, in writing the part.

STRINGS

SONATA IN C MAJOR
Haydn

Viola

SONATA IN B MINOR
Liszt

Viola

SONATA PATHÉTIQUE, OP. 13
Beethoven

Cello

ETUDE, OP. 25, No. 7
Chopin

Cello

SONATA, OP. 10, No. 2
Beethoven

Double Bass

STRINGS

Exercises in Bowing and in the Use of Alto and Tenor Clefs

The following fragments are given with the phrasing or slurring used in the original (piano) version. Write each passage on the staff below it and add bowing indications—slurs, up-bow and down-bow signs where necessary, etc. Aim at the effect of the original. In the exercise for the double bass, be sure to write the part an octave higher than the concert sounds shown.

STRINGS

Following are fragments from orchestral works with bowing slurs deleted. Add slurs and any other appropriate bowing indications. Then refer, via the index, to the full-score examples of the same measures given in the text and inspect the bowing specified by the composers. If your version differs from the latter, that does not necessarily mean that it is "wrong." This exercise (which will not be graded), simply aims to acquaint students with bowing patterns considered most effective by composers, in particular musical situations.

© 1910 Editions Max Eschig. Used by Permission. Sole Representative U.S.A. Theodore Presser Company.

Used by permission of copyright owner, Lee Roberts Music Publications, Inc.

STRINGS

Include bowing indications. The instructor should discuss the voice-leading in measures 5 and 6.

SONATA IN B♭ MAJOR

August Eberhard Müller

STRINGS

SONATA IN B♭ MAJOR (continued)

STRINGS

Exercise in Error Detection (String Scoring)

The scoring here contains a number of errors that occur frequently in students' first work in arranging for strings. On this sheet (or orally in class) point out the errors. Score the excerpt for strings if the instructor so directs.

STRINGS

Score for strings. Analyze the voice-leading carefully before beginning the scoring. Division of the cellos (half on the lower octave of the inner-voice melody and half on the bass) will be necessary in mm. 1–8; there the two lines are best written on separate staves. Divisi passages in other string groups may be written on the same staff.

ROMANZE, OP. 118, NO. 5

Brahms

Score for strings.

Score for strings. The instructor should discuss the voice leading and a suitable scoring of the rolled chords in measures 6 and 7.

STRINGS

Score for strings. Analyze first, noting important melodic elements that recur.

ARIA
from "Five Piano Pieces"

Peter Mennin

STRINGS

Exercises in Writing Multiple Stops

In Exercise A score the given chords for strings using multiple stops. The numbers in parentheses indicate the number of notes to be used in each multiple stop. Do not add or omit pitches (though pitches may be duplicated). The charts in Chapter 2 of the text may be consulted for practical multiple-stop patterns. Make use of open strings where possible and aim at fullness of sound.

The chords in Exercise B have been extracted from Beethoven's symphonies. Write them for strings using multiple stops (chiefly triple stops in the violins).

For Exercise C use a separate sheet of music paper and score the passage for strings using multiple stops. The last two chords may be lifted and respaced.

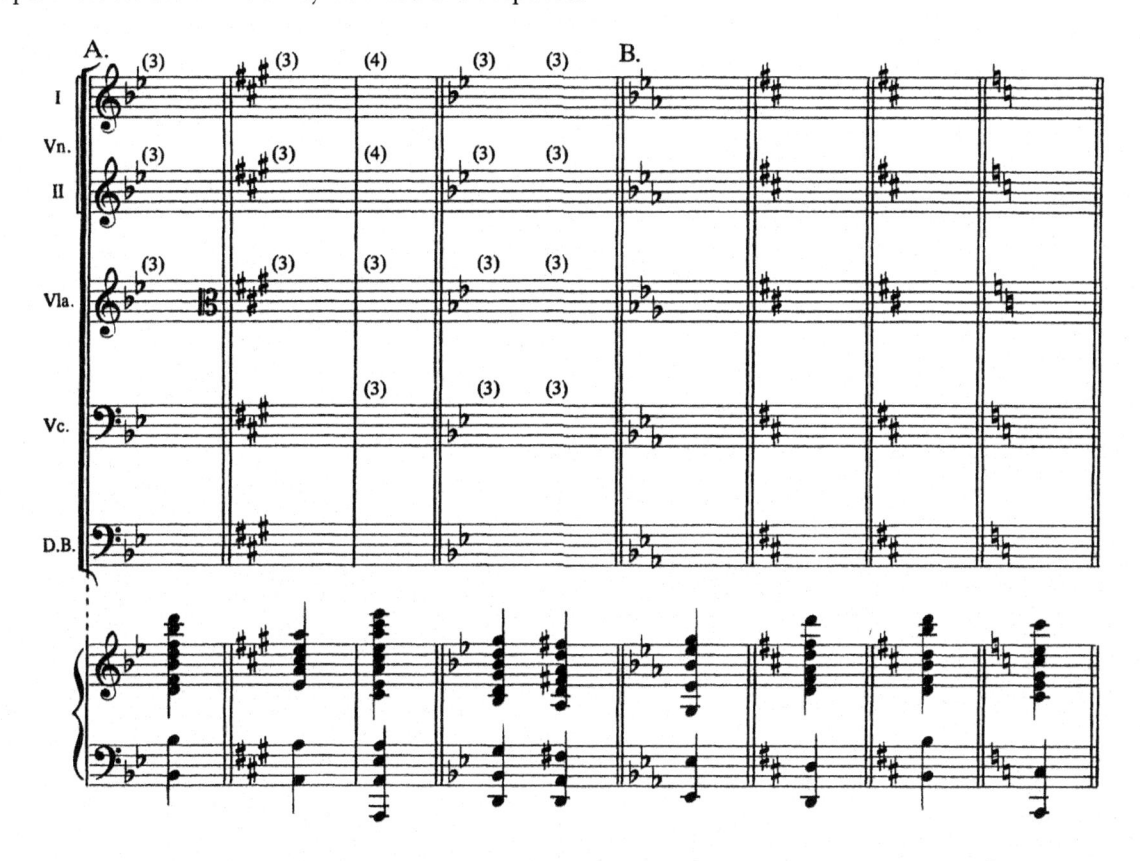

STRINGS

Exercises in Reading and in Notating String Harmonics

In A, show on the staff below the given harmonics how each will sound. Remember that the double bass sounds an octave lower than written, even in harmonics—except when written in treble clef, in which case it is intended to sound as written.

In B, write the given concert pitches as harmonics, showing all the possibilities for each even though some are much more likely than others to be used. (In each case as many spaces are provided as there are possibilities.) Include both natural and artificial harmonics for the violin and the viola but only natural harmonics for the cello and the double bass.

In C, show beside each chord how the individual notes will sound.

* The original notation also includes the pitches of the resulting harmonics. These are omitted here for purposes of this exercise.

Ex.C1: © Copyright 1929 by Editions Russes de Musique. Copyright Renewed. Copyright and Renewal Assigned to Boosey & Hawkes, Inc. Used by permission. Ex. C2: Copyright 1907 Durand S.A. Editions Musicales, 1981. Editions ARIMA and Durand S.A. Theodore Presser Company, Sole Representative U.S.A. Ex. C3: © Copyright 1961 by Universal Edition A.G. Wien. Copyright Renewed. All rights reserved. Used by permission of European American Music Distributors Corporation, sole U.S. and Canadian agent for Universal Edition.

STRINGS

Score Study: Fantasia on *"Greensleeves"*
Ralph Vaughan Williams

Below is a standard four-part harmonization of the English folksong *Greensleeves*.

Greensleeves
Traditional

This version could have been scored in many of the ways described in Chapter 3 of *The Technique of Orchestration* on pp. 32–37, but Ralph Vaughan Williams scored it in a more distinctive and original way in his *Fantasia on "Greensleeves."* (Williams includes another English folksong, *Lovely Joan,* as the B section of this work.)

After listening to a recording while following the score, answer the following questions concerning *Fantasia on "Greensleeves."*

STRINGS

FANTASIA ON 'GREENSLEEVES'

For String Orchestra and Harp (or Pianoforte), with 1 or 2 optional Flutes

Arranged from the score of the Opera by
RALPH GREAVES

R. VAUGHAN WILLIAMS
Adapted from the Opera
'Sir John in Love'

12
Harp
Vln I
Vln II
Vla
Vc
DB
Solo arco
Tutti pizz.

18
Harp
Vln I
Vln II
Vla
Vc
DB
Solo arco

*Folk tune "Lovely Joan"

35
Vln I
Vln II
Vla
Vc
DB
unis.
unis.
40
Fl I or Solo Vln
Fl II or Solo Vln
Vln I
Vln II
Vla I
Vla II
Vc I
Vc II
DB
p
p
pizz.
p
pizz.
p
unis.
div.
(2nd ½ desks)
pizz.
(pizz.)
(pizz.)
div.
(2nd ½ desks)
pizz.
(pizz.)
(pizz.)

STRINGS

STRINGS

STRINGS

STRINGS

86
Harp
Vln I
Vln II
Vla
Vc I
Vc II
DB

90
Harp
Vln I
pp
Vln II
pp
Vla
ppp
Vc I
ppp
arco
Vc II
ppp
DB

STRINGS

1. Examine the spacing between the Fl and the low strings in m. 1. Why do you think the composer restricted the register of the strings?

2. Why is it practical to write Vln II on two staves?

3. In what instruments does the melody appear beginning in m. 8? What is the interval of the doubling? Where does the upper octave presentation of the melody occur in relation to the other violin parts?

4. Examine the different ways the dotted-eighth/sixteenth figures are bowed in the melody in mm. 8–23. Consider the different effect of each.

5. How does the Vc chord in m. 8 differ from the chord in m. 11? What instruments do the Vc complement?

6. What *exact* special effect is called for in m. 24 in Vln II and Vla?

7. Identify the three different textural elements that occur in mm. 8–23. What textural change occurs in m. 24?

8. Why is the "Tutti pizz." indication necessary in mm. 17 and 24?

9. For what practical reason does the composer ask for 1/2 desks only in Vla and Vc in m. 32?

10. Discuss the bowing in mm. 32 to 36 in Vla and Vc. Be as specific as you can about all of the composer's marks.

11. What major textural/register change occurs at m. 32?

12. What bowing is suggested by the markings in mm. 48–57 in the lower strings? What do you hear in the recording you listened to—on the string, off the string?

13. How many different voices are there at the pickup to m. 49 and following? Describe the texture.

14. Compare mm. 68 and following with mm. 8 and following. What happens? How do they differ?

15. From earlier in the piece, what is the source of the Vla part that occurs in mm. 75 and 83?

16. What is the interval of doubling between Vla and Vc at mm. 76–83?

17. Find the analogous point to m. 84 in the first third of the piece. How is the scoring different? Why is the scoring at m. 84 a better choice of the two to end the work?

18. What do you find of interest in the chord spacing in the final two bars?

WOODWINDS
Chapters 5, 6

Exercises in the Notation of Transposing Woodwinds

These exercises involve two types of transposition. In some cases the actual (concert) sounds are given, and the passage is to be notated in transposed form on the staff above it, with the appropriate key signature. In other cases, the passage is given as it appears in the orchestral score and is to be written on the staff below as it will actually sound—again with a key signature, except in the case of the Stravinsky excerpt, which uses none in the original.

WOODWINDS

SECOND SYMPHONY
Schumann

FIFTH SYMPHONY
Dvořák

CAPRICCIO ESPAGNOL
Rimsky-Korsakoff

GÖTTERDÄMMERUNG
Wagner

THE RITE OF SPRING
Stravinsky

FIRST SYMPHONY
Mahler

SCHELOMO
Bloch

Copyright renewal assigned, 1945, to G. Schirmer, Inc. Used by permission.

Exercise in Error Detection (Woodwind Scoring)

The scoring here contains a number of errors that occur frequently in students' first work in arranging for woodwinds. In the blanks at the bottom of the page, list the error or errors that occur at each corresponding circled number in the music. Points to look for include omission or incorrect use of "1." or "2." or "a2," instruments written out of their range, poor balance, failure to transpose the part, rests missing, linear flaws, etc. This exercise may be done orally in class but in any case should be undertaken before the first assignment in scoring for woodwinds.

1.
2.
3.
4.
5.
6.
7.
8.
9.
10.
11.
12.
13.
14.
15.
16.
17.
18.

Score for woodwinds in pairs.

SONATA, OP. 122
Schubert

First look over the entire piece, noting any passages that will have to be taken by particular instruments because of the range involved. Then plot the scoring. In bars 9–16, use quarter notes or dotted half notes in the bottom voice in order to approximate the sustained effect that the pedal gives in the piano version.

SONATINA, OP. 55, No. 4

Kuhlau

WOODWINDS

SONATINA, OP. 55, NO. 4 (continued)

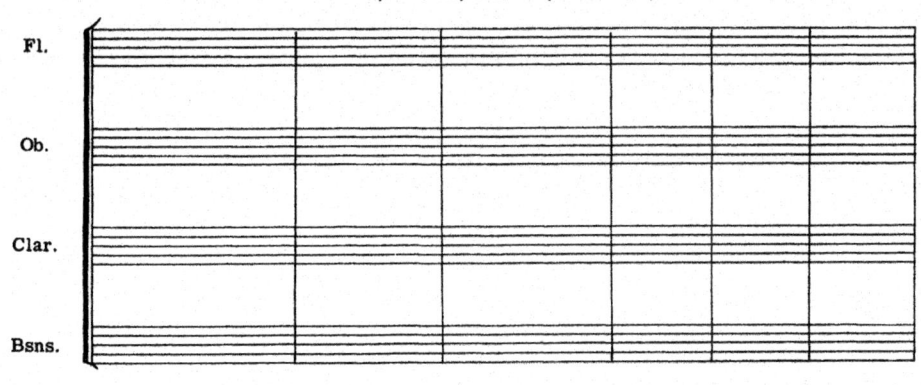

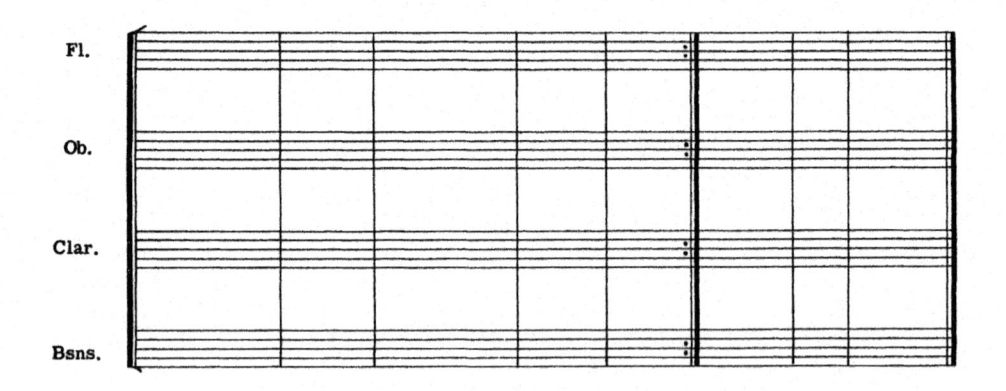

Score for woodwinds in pairs.

SONATA, OP. 2, NO. 3

Score for woodwinds in pairs.

No. 21 From LITTLE PIECES FOR CHILDREN, Vol. 1

Bartók

WOODWINDS

Expand the original version by doubling the soprano and bass an octave lower and the soprano, alto, and tenor an octave higher. (The upper-octave doubling of the soprano in the piccolo will sound two octaves higher than in the original.) On another sheet, sketch the scoring of the first measure or so at actual pitch before writing the orchestration in transposed form on this page.

CHRISTUS, DER IST MEIN LEBEN

J. S. Bach

Piccolo

2 Flutes

2 Oboes

English Horn

2 Clarinets in

Bass Clarinet

2 Bassoons

Contra Bassoon

WOODWINDS

Score for flute, oboe, English horn, clarinet, bass clarinet, and bassoon. This piece is also suitable for an assignment in scoring for strings.

FUGA SECUNDA IN G
From
Ludus Tonalis

Hindemith

II
(GIUOCO DELLE COPPIE)

WOODWINDS

WOODWINDS

WOODWINDS

WOODWINDS

41

WOODWINDS

WOODWINDS

WOODWINDS

WOODWINDS

WOODWINDS

Score Study: Concerto for Orchestra, Second Movement
Bela Bartók

1. "Giuoco delle Coppie" translates as "Game of Pairs," and this movement begins with five duets for wind instruments. Each duet is played by a pair of the same instrument, and that instrument plays *only* its duet in this section of the piece. None of the instruments playing these duets are identified in the score below. Based upon your reading of Chapter 5 in *The Technique of Orchestration* by Kent Kennan and Donald Grantham, decide what pair of instruments is likely playing the duet at each of the numbered entries on the score. Give one or two reasons for each choice.

2. Comment on and contrast the articulations used for the different pairs.

3. Examine the intervallic content of each of the duets. What do you observe?

4. Comment on the articulation at letter *a*.

5. How is the *pizz.* to be performed at letter *b*?

6. How is Violin II instructed to play the material at letter *c*?

7. How does the quadruple stop in the Vla at letter *d* relate to the other string parts?

8. Are the triple-stop chords at letter *e* practical for a Vc section?

9. What is unusual about the rhythmic notation of the duet at number *3*? How does this relate to the material in this duet?

10. What is called for in Vln I at letter *f*? How does this differ from what is called for in Vln I in the preceding three measures?

11. At letter *g*, identify the string each harmonic would be played on and the harmonic number of each of the harmonics.

12. To what is the material at letter *h* related?

13. How is the material at letter *i* related to the other material in the strings?

14. Why might Bartók have offered the alternate version in the Fls at letter *j*?

15. What kind of articulation is called for in the Fls at letter *k*?

16. Why is the interlocking at letter *l* in Vln II and Vla a better alternative than juxtaposition?

17. What special effect is Bartók calling for at letter *m*?

18. What is indicated at letter *n*?

19. Examine each chord in the strings at letter *o*. What kind of harmony is used? What kind of harmony is used for each chord in the strings at letter *p*?

20. Comment on the trumpet parts at letter *q*. What is a practical reason for the use of trumpet 3 here?

BRASS
Chapters 7, 8, 9

Exercise in Converting Parts for Horns and Trumpets in Various Keys to Concert Pitches

Below each of the following excerpts from orchestral horn and trumpet parts write the passage as it will actually sound. Include a key signature except in the case of the Strauss and Scriabin examples. This exercise does not attempt to exhaust all the key possibilities for horns and trumpets; but it does include those most often encountered in the study of orchestral scores of the past.

BRASS

OVERTURE TO THE MARRIAGE OF FIGARO
Mozart

Horns in D

LEONORE No. 3 OVERTURE
Beethoven

Horns in C

VARIATIONS ON A THEME OF HAYDN
Brahms

Horns in B♭ basso

SYMPHONY
Franck

Trumpets in F

DON JUAN
Strauss

Trumpets in E

POEM OF ECSTASY
Scriabin

Trumpets in B♭

OVERTURE TO OBERON
Weber

Trumpets in D

BRASS

Score the chorale excerpt below for each of the brass groups shown. In the case of the third one, base the scoring on the "expanded version," which achieves greater fullness by doubling the soprano and the bass at the lower octave.

O HAUPT VOLL BLUT UND WUNDEN

J. S. Bach

BRASS

Transpose to a higher key and double the melody and bass an octave lower. Make a preliminary sketch of the scoring in the new key, on the staves provided for that purpose.

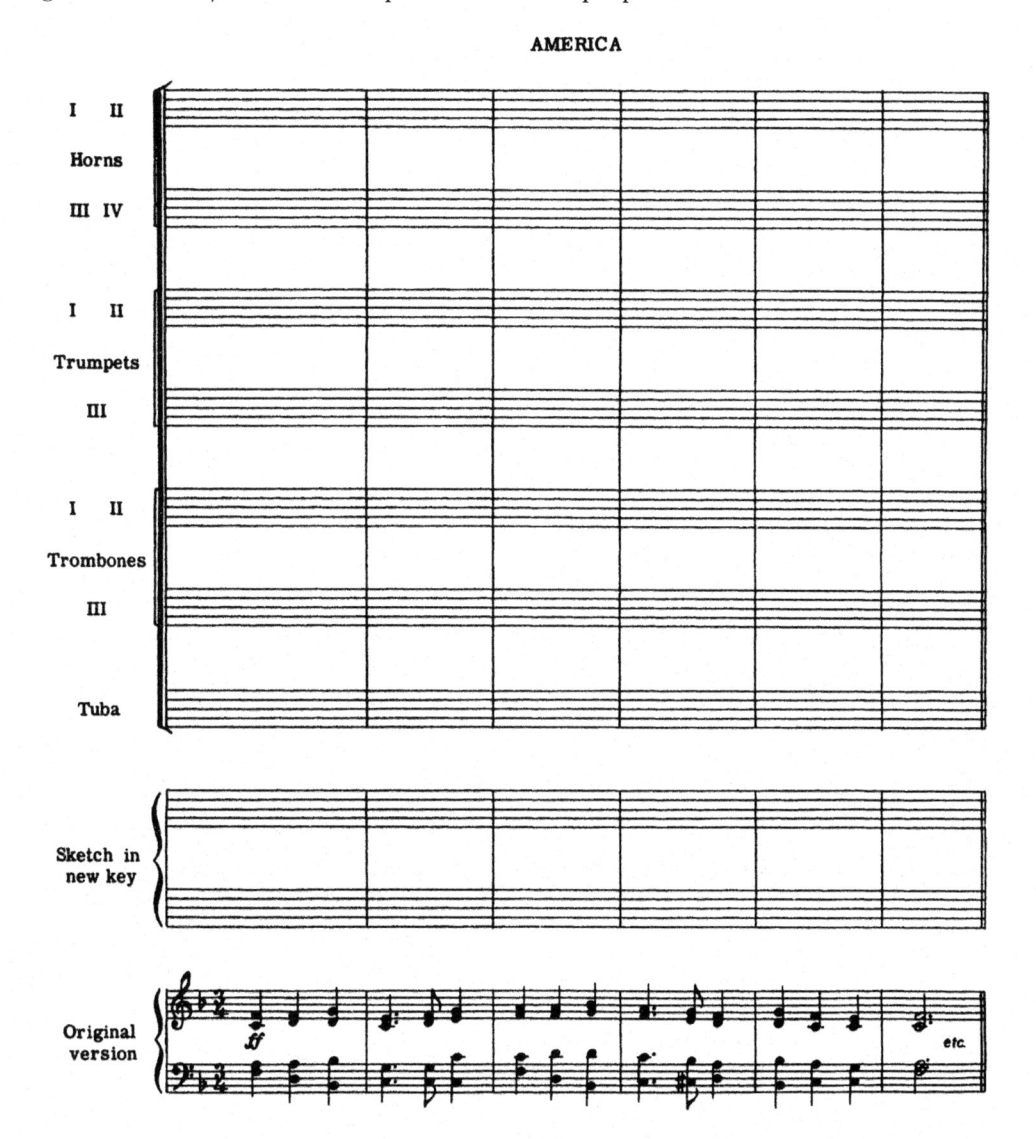

AMERICA

BRASS

Score for two horns, two B♭ trumpets, and two trombones.

DAMON AND PHILLIS
From
Canzonets or Little Short Airs
to Five and Six Voices*

Morley

* Words omitted here

BRASS

Score for brass (four horns, two trumpets, three trombones, and tuba).

SAILOR'S SONG

Grieg

Allegro vivace e marcato

BRASS

Score for brass (two or four horns, two trumpets, three trombones, tuba). Transposition of the piece down a half step results in a more comfortable key for B♭ trumpets but detracts somewhat from the brilliant effect. If the original key is retained and if B♭ trumpets are used, their part should be spelled enharmonically from measure 8 on.

This excerpt is also suitable for an assignment in scoring for orchestra.

WAR SONG
From
Album for the Young

Schumann

Score for brass (four horns, three trumpets, three trombones, tuba). Compare your completed scoring with Ravel's. This excerpt is also suitable for an assignment in scoring for orchestra.

PROMENADE
From
Pictures at an Exhibition

Mussorgsky

Score for brass (four horns, three trumpets, three trombones, tuba). Consider the use of mutes. This piece is also suitable for an assignment in scoring for woodwinds, horns, and strings.

FOLK SONG No. 8
From
Ten Easy Pieces for Piano

Bartók

SCORING OF CHORDS
Chapter 10

Chords for Orchestra, Score Study

The following questions pertain to Example 10.13 found on pp. 181–185 of the textbook. Not all of these questions have a definitive answer. Some are intended to promote reflection and discussion.

Example 10.13g

1. What interval is emphasized in this chord? How is this accomplished?

2. What triad member is least represented, and where does it occur?

3. Which of the four ways in which instruments can be combined is most used? (See Example 10.1, p. 172.)

4. How many open strings are playable in Vln I and II? In Vla? In Vc?

5. Comment on the relative position of the three sections in this chord.

Example 10.13h

1. What less common instrument is called for in this chord?

2. What method of combination is used in the trombones and horns?

3. Comment on the relative placement of the clarinets in this *tutti* chord at this dynamic, as compared with more modern scorings (see examples i and l).

4. Is the bass clarinet used in a conventional and effective way?

SCORING OF CHORDS

5. Compare this chord with 10.13g, from a symphony written about 80 years earlier.

Pay particular attention to the size of the orchestra and the instrumentation, differences in spacing, differences/similarities in the use of juxtaposition, overlapping, ranges, and disposition of the strings, etc.

Example 10.13i

1. What Roman numeral would identify this chord in F major?

2. What chord member is not represented in the upper voicing? Why not?

3. What unusual/less common instrument does Strauss call for? What instrument would play this part today?

4. Comment on the relative placement of the string and woodwind sections to the brass section. What advantage does Strauss's arrangement have?

Example 10.13j

1. Describe the aural effect created by the scoring on the downbeat of this *ff* chord, considering the relative weight of the three sections.

2. What makes the sustaining winds sound "dark"?

3. Could the bass clarinet have played the lowest note? If so, why might Wagner have chosen to use the bassoon rather than the bass clarinet for the lowest note?

Example 10.13k

1. Examine the scoring of the woodwinds. What chord member has Wagner chosen to emphasize, and how? Describe the spacing in the woodwinds.

2. Describe and comment on the placement of the brass instruments.

3. Would this placement of the sections have worked in a *ff* chord? Why or why not?

SCORING OF CHORDS

Example 10.13l

1. Comment on the distribution/spacing of the woodwind and string sections. Why are they arranged like this?

2. What instrument does the English horn reinforce? In examining the brass, why is this a good choice?

3. What other instruments is the piano associated with?

Example 10.13m

1. Where is the most dissonant element of this chord located, and how is it scored?

2. Which instruments play flutter-tongued? What other instrument complements this effect?

Example 10.13n

1. What is the lowest pitch in this chord? The highest?

2. What instruments play primarily in the fourth octave (C4–C5)? Where do the other sections play in relation to these instruments and why?

3. Comment on the trumpet scoring.

4. Comment on the bassoon scoring. What instruments are they paired with?

Example 10.13o

1. What is the lowest pitch in this chord? The highest?

2. Describe and comment on the scoring of the low dyad.

3. Comment on the use of the clarinets (note their register).

4. Comment on the scoring of the brass section. Is it more or less traditional?

5. Comment on the spacing in the woodwind section.

SCORING OF CHORDS

These chords are given in basic four-voice form. In scoring them, octave doublings are to be added wherever appropriate, but the chord members now in bass and soprano should be retained; for example, in the second chord below, a G (in whatever octave is desired) should be the top note, and a C should be the bottom note. In scoring brass, be sure to observe the principles of balance discussed in the text.

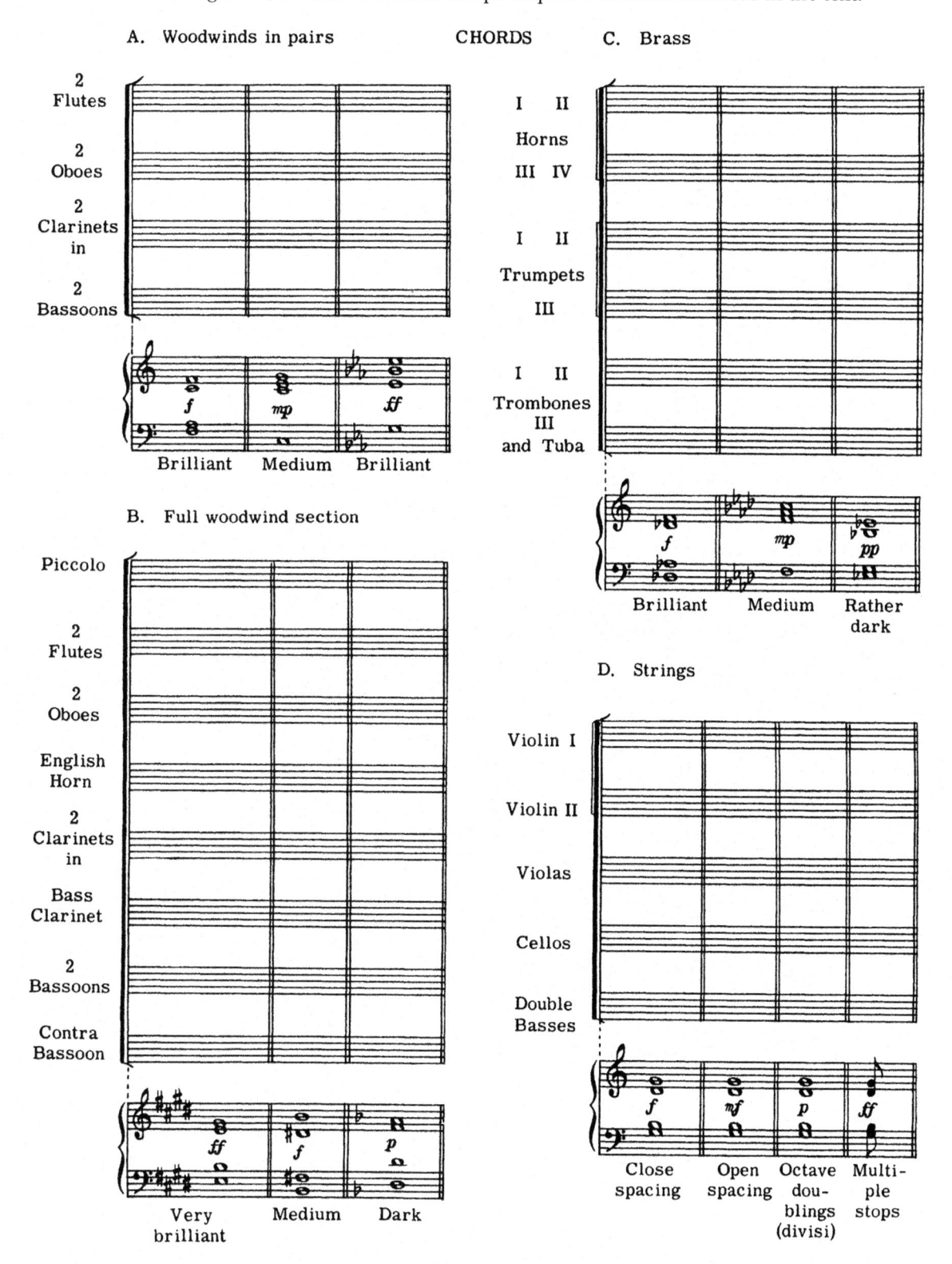

CHORDS

A. Woodwinds in pairs

2 Flutes
2 Oboes
2 Clarinets in
2 Bassoons

Brilliant — Medium — Brilliant

B. Full woodwind section

Piccolo
2 Flutes
2 Oboes
English Horn
2 Clarinets in
Bass Clarinet
2 Bassoons
Contra Bassoon

Very brilliant — Medium — Dark

C. Brass

Horns I II / III IV
Trumpets I II / III
Trombones I II / III and Tuba

Brilliant — Medium — Rather dark

D. Strings

Violin I
Violin II
Violas
Cellos
Double Basses

Close spacing — Open spacing — Octave doublings (divisi) — Multiple stops

SCORING OF CHORDS

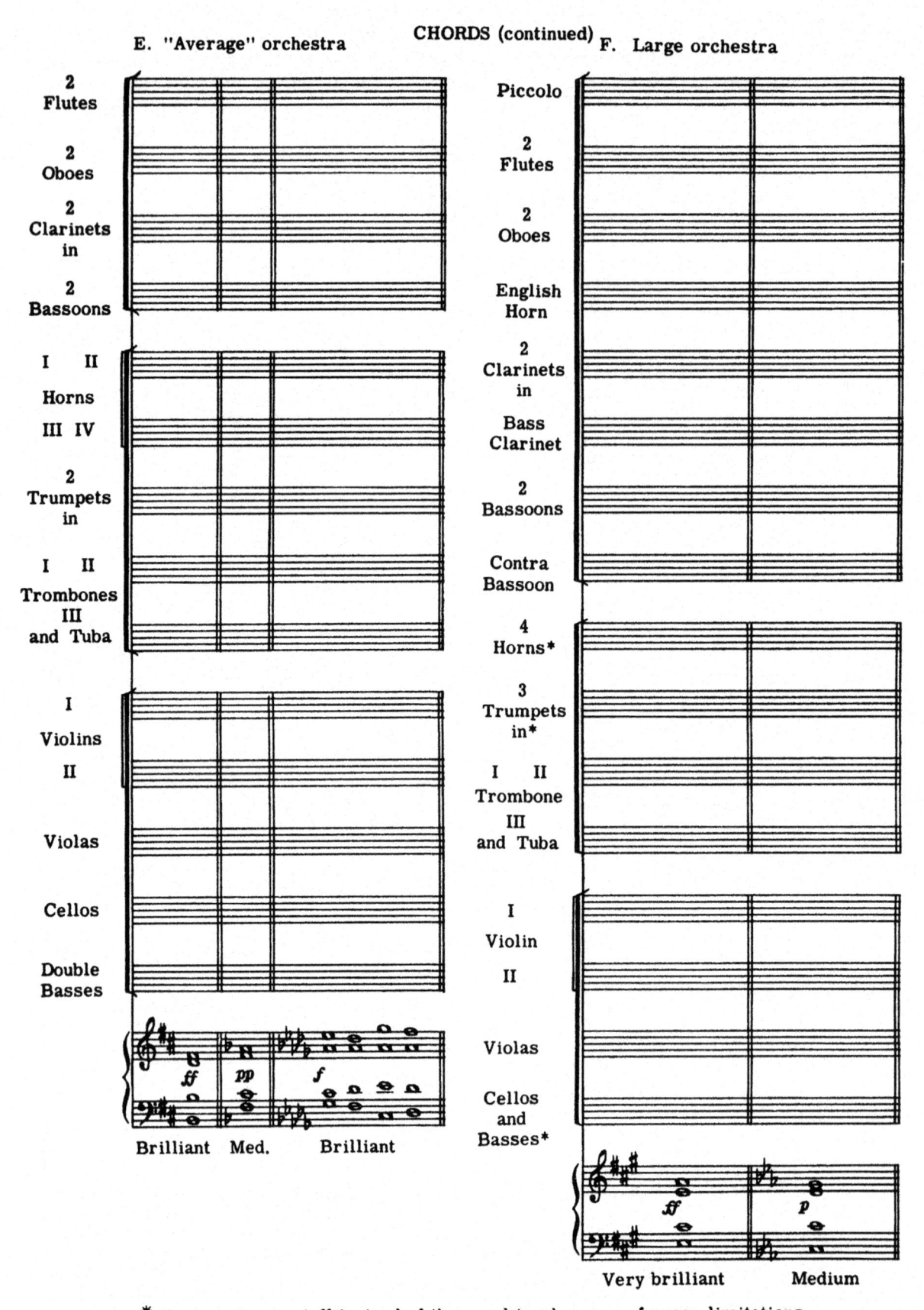

CHORDS (continued)

E. "Average" orchestra

- 2 Flutes
- 2 Oboes
- 2 Clarinets in
- 2 Bassoons
- Horns I II, III IV
- 2 Trumpets in
- Trombones I II, III and Tuba
- Violins I, II
- Violas
- Cellos
- Double Basses

Brilliant — Med. — Brilliant

F. Large orchestra

- Piccolo
- 2 Flutes
- 2 Oboes
- English Horn
- 2 Clarinets in
- Bass Clarinet
- 2 Bassoons
- Contra Bassoon
- 4 Horns*
- 3 Trumpets in*
- Trombone I II, III and Tuba
- Violin I, II
- Violas
- Cellos and Basses*

Very brilliant — Medium

* Written on one staff instead of the usual two because of space limitations.

SCORING OF CHORDS

These chords are given in basic four-voice form, some with a key signature and some with accidentals instead. When a key signature is used in the original version, write the appropriate key signature in the part for each instrument; when no key signature appears in the original, use none in the scored version but write in accidentals. Chords in open spacing should be converted to close spacing in the scored versions, and octave doublings are to be added wherever appropriate. The chord members now in bass and soprano should be retained; for example, in the third chord below, a D (in whatever octave is desired) should be the bottom note, and a B should be the top note. In the exercises on the next page, an extra staff is provided as an aid in sketching the chords in advance.

61

SCORING OF CHORDS

D. "Average" orchestra   E. Large orchestra

Brilliant   Dark   Medium   Medium   Very brilliant

PROBLEMS IN TRANSCRIBING PIANO MUSIC
Chapter 11

Transcribing Piano Music for Orchestra, Score Study

The following questions pertain to Examples 11.21–11.24 found on pp. 198–205 of the textbook. The original piano music is shown below the orchestrated version for each example in the textbook.

Example 11.21a

1. Comment on the phrasing/articulation in the piano part. Is this maintained in the orchestration?

2. What is unusual about the horns called for by Ravel? What is the *Cor simple*?

3. What new element is presented in the winds? What function does this serve?

4. What type of chord arrangement is used in the winds (see Example 10.1)?

5. How does the treatment of the eighth notes in the piano differ from the scoring in the orchestra? Why did Ravel do this?

6. What advantage can you see to scoring the bass line in the low strings as Ravel does?

Example 11.21b

1. How is the melody scored? What is another way the pairs of flutes and clarinets could have been scored? What would be the aural difference between these two ways?

2. What is the material in Vln I related to in Example 11.21a? Comment on the bowing of the upper half of Vln I (bear in mind the tempo).

3. Explain exactly how the divisi in Vln ll works.

DOI: 10.4324/9781003130697-5

4. Would the multiple stops in Vla and Vc work a half-step higher? A half-step lower?

5. What is Ravel asking for in measure 2, beat 2 in the Vla?

Example 11.21c

1. Comment on the scoring of Fl 2.

2. Comment on the different phrasing between flutes and Vln I and Vln II. Would the Fl phrasing be a good bowing for the Vlns?

3. Why is it unnecessary for the Vc to provide more than one note on the weak beats of each measure?

4. Discuss the scoring of the bass line compared with the piano.

Example 11.22a

1. What is the purpose of the violin parts in the pickup to the first measure?

2. What instruments play a similar role in mm. 1, 2, and 3? (Numbering begins with the first complete measure.) What bowing is indicated for this material?

3. What is Ravel asking for in the Vc on the strong beats?

4. Should Vln II take an up-bow or a down-bow on the downbeats of mm. 2 and 3? Why?

5. What are the sounding pitches for the double harmonics in the Vla? On what strings would these harmonics be played?

6. What is the sounding pitch for the harmonic in the VC in m. 3?

7. Comment on the dynamics in piano vs. orchestra.

PROBLEMS IN TRANSCRIBING

Example 11.22b

1. What do you consider to be the most striking difference between the piano and the orchestration? Why is this difference necessary and called for?

2. Explain how the melodic line is scored and how the scoring reinforces what is indicated in the piano.

3. How is the DB part different from most 18th- and 19th-century DB parts?

4. Why are the Vln II and Vla parts divided differently in mm. 3 and 4, since they're playing the same thing one octave apart?

5. What are the sounding pitches for the harmonics in the Vc part? Could the pitches given in the piano part be played as harmonics by the Vc?

6. What kind of chord arrangement is used in the Ob/Eh/Cls?

7. Discuss the difference in dynamics between the piano and orchestra versions.

Example 11.23a

1. What special effect is called for in the left hand of the piano in m. 2? (Note the asterisk and the footnote.)

2. Which instruments recreate the above special effect in the orchestration? What special effects does Copland specify for these instruments?

3. Examine the scoring of the theme in the first two bars. Why do you think Copland calls for the different rhythmic values?

4. Compare the instruments that play con sordino and those that don't. What seems to determine which instruments are or are not muted?

5. Compare the piano chord on beat two of measure 3 with the scoring of the chord in the orchestra. Are there any pitch additions or omissions?

PROBLEMS IN TRANSCRIBING

Example 11.23b

1. What advantage do the grace notes in the strings have over an attempt to score the grace notes exactly as they occur in the piano? What do the tied notes in the strings reflect in the piano original?

2. What is the source of the chord in the Bsns, Hrns, Trb 3, and DB?

3. What do the triplets in the woodwinds add to the texture?

4. Discuss the scoring of the quarter note lines.

5. Which orchestral instruments are capable of playing the last note in the piano in the same octave?

Example 11.23c

1. What notational change occurs between the piano and the orchestral versions? What practical advantage does this change achieve?

2. How many different ways is the left-hand part scored? Describe them.

3. In how many octaves does the right-hand part occur in the first two measures in the woodwinds? In the strings?

4. What is the source of the horn and trombone parts in the first two bars? What effect does this have on the overall texture?

5. What change occurs in the trombone parts from the first to the second bar?

6. In what rhythm is the timpani playing? What part is it complementing?

7. What is one advantage of scoring the horns as they are in mm. 3–5? (What would the Hrn 1 and 3 parts look like if they had continued playing the entire line?)

PROBLEMS IN TRANSCRIBING

Example 11.24a

1. What other orchestral instruments could have played the opening gesture of this piece?

2. What dynamic ambiguity occurs in the brass in mm. 2–4? If you were the conductor what information would you need to supply for the brass?

3. What instruction is given to the trumpets in mm. 5–6?

4. Rochberg divides the trichords in the final three measures between horns and trombones. Could any of the brass have played the entire three bars alone? If so, which would be the more effective?

5. To what extent are octave doublings employed in this excerpt?

Score for strings (or for any other combination of instruments specified by the instructor). Rearrange, fill, etc. wherever appropriate. Including bowing indications.

This excerpt used by permission of Breitkopf & Haertel, Leipzig–Associated Music Publishers, Inc.

SONATA, K. 330 above is written as the third of a group of three sonatas (K. 330 in C, K. 331 in A, and K. 332 in F).

Score for strings (or for any other combination of instruments specified by the instructor). Rearrange, fill, etc. wherever appropriate. Include bowing indications.

PROBLEMS IN TRANSCRIBING

Score for strings. Rearrange, fill, etc. wherever appropriate. Include bowing indications.

SONATA, OP. 22
Beethoven

SCORING FOR WOODWINDS, HORNS, AND STRINGS
Chapter 12

Scoring for Woodwinds, Horns, and Strings, Score Study

The following questions pertain to Examples 12.6–12.11 found on pp. 216–222 of the textbook. Not all of these questions have a definitive answer. Some are intended to promote reflection and discussion.

Example 12.6

1. Arrange this excerpt so that it is playable at the piano. (You can do this by concentrating on the strings.)

2. Comment on the scoring and octave placement of the melody. Comment on any differences in the scoring of the melody in the various instruments. Where does the melody occur in relation to the other parts?

3. Comment on the role of the Vla. Comment on the space the Vla occupies in relation to the other instruments. What kind of bowing is called for in the Vla?

4. How would you characterize the bowing in Vln I in mm. 6 and 7 as compared with the first two measures?

5. Comment on the use of the Vc and DB. What instruments partially double the bass?

6. Where do the horns sound in relation to the written pitches?

Example 12.7

1. Comment on the instrumentation required by Schubert. (The full instrumentation is included in this excerpt.)

2. Where do the horns sound in relation to the written pitches?

3. Comment on the scoring for Vlas, Vc, and DB in mm. 1–6. Will the Vla be able to employ its open D string? Why or why not?

4. What does the bowing in the Vlns tend to emphasize in the first four bars? What does that complement in the other parts?

5. Comment on the orchestral texture in the last four bars. Why do the horns have a different version of what everyone else has? What would the horns have to do to play the complete line?

Example 12.8

1. Where do the horns sound in relation to the written pitches? What kind of horn do you think is required here? Why?

2. How many horns are required in mm. 3–5? How do you know?

3. Comment on the scoring of the oboes and bassoons in mm. 1–10. The strings in mm. 1–10.

4. Why is the DB line altered in mm. 7–10?

5. Comment on the slurring in the woodwinds in mm. 1–10. The slurring/bowing in mm. 1–10 in low strings.

6. Comment on the scoring of the woodwinds in mm. 11–14. What is an advantage of scoring the woodwinds in this fashion?

7. Comment on the scoring of the strings in mm. 11–14. Where does this material come from?

Examples 12.9a, 12.9b

1. Discuss and compare the scoring of the melody on pp. 219 and 220.

2. Discuss the scoring of the bass line on pp. 219 and 220.

3. What kind of bowing is called for in the upper strings on p. 219?

4. Discuss the arrangement of the string chords in the first two bars of p. 219 and compare this to bars 3 and 4. What happens?

5. In how many octaves does the melody occur on p. 220?

6. Discuss the scoring of the triplets in the woodwinds and horns on p. 220. What does the slurring in flute 1, oboes and clarinets complement in the other woodwinds and horns?

7. Discuss the scoring of flutes 2 and 3, oboes, and clarinets on p. 220.

Example 12.10

1. Prokofiev entitled this work Classical Symphony. What are some characteristics of this excerpt that justify this title?

2. Discuss the scoring and the doubling of the melody throughout the entire excerpt.

3. How does Prokofiev add a little extra color and emphasis to the downbeat of mm. 5 and 7? (Numbering of measures begins with the first complete bar.)

4. Would up-bow or down-bow be more appropriate in Vln I and Vc in the last half of m. 8? Why?

Example 12.11

1. Note the instrumentation of this work; there is only one player per part. Note also the tempo.

2. Comment on the Vc pizz. in the first four bars. To what other parts is it related?

3. Why does Britten specify up-bow in Vln 1 in m. 3 and Vla in m. 5?

4. To what other parts is the horn related? Why is it wise for the horn to provide only a partial doubling?

5. Comment on the use of the DB.

6. Discuss the doubling of the lowest part of the texture beginning in m. 7.

7. What parts complement the high woodwinds beginning in m. 7? How do these complementary parts differ?

SCORING FOR WOODWINDS

In planning the scoring, take into account the antiphonal effect at the beginning.

SONATA, OP. 90
Beethoven

SCORING FOR WOODWINDS

SONATA, OP. 90 (continued)

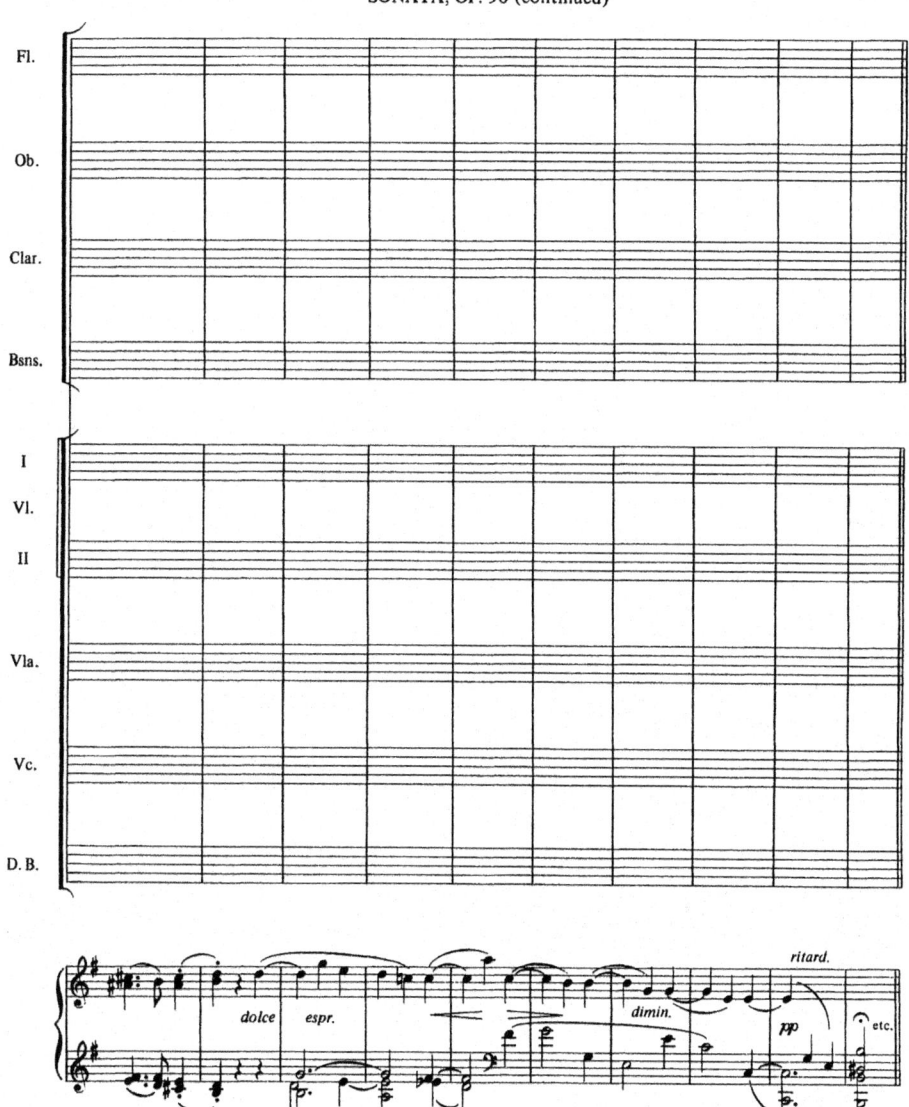

SCORING FOR WOODWINDS

Score for woodwinds, horns, and strings. In the repeat of the first twelve measures, vary the scoring and add upper-octave doublings. From measure 33 on, partially fill in the wide gap between the hands. This piece is also suitable as an exercise in scoring for an orchestra that includes full brass and timpani.

AT CHURCH

Tchaikovsky

SCORING FOR WOODWINDS

Score the excerpt below in four different ways (versions 3 and 4 on the reverse side). Use only the instruments desired in each version—except for number 4, which is to use all the instruments listed. Include octave doublings of the melody in at least two versions. In addition to these actual scorings, describe two other possible scorings in the space provided on the next page.

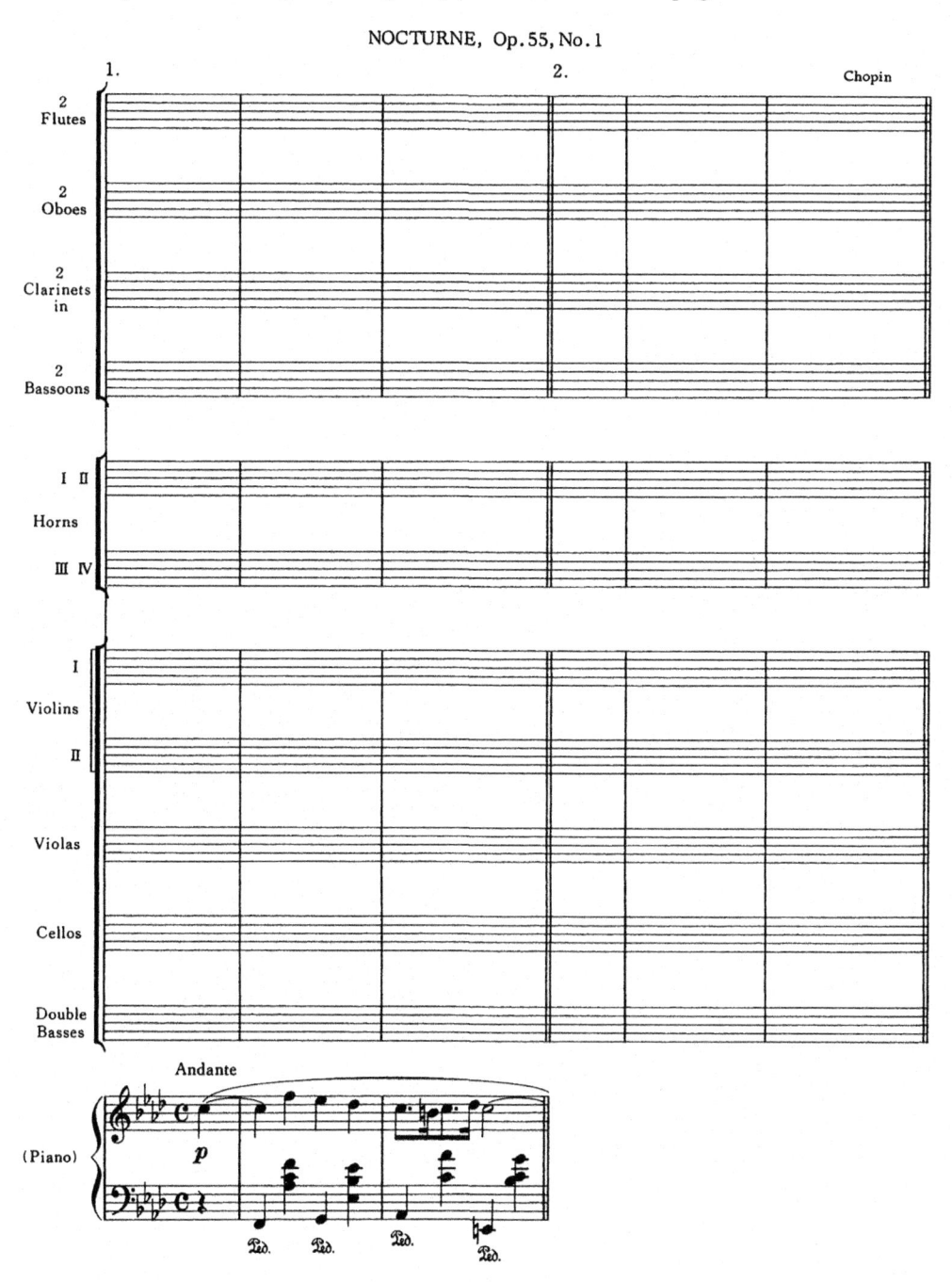

NOCTURNE, Op. 55, No. 1

Chopin

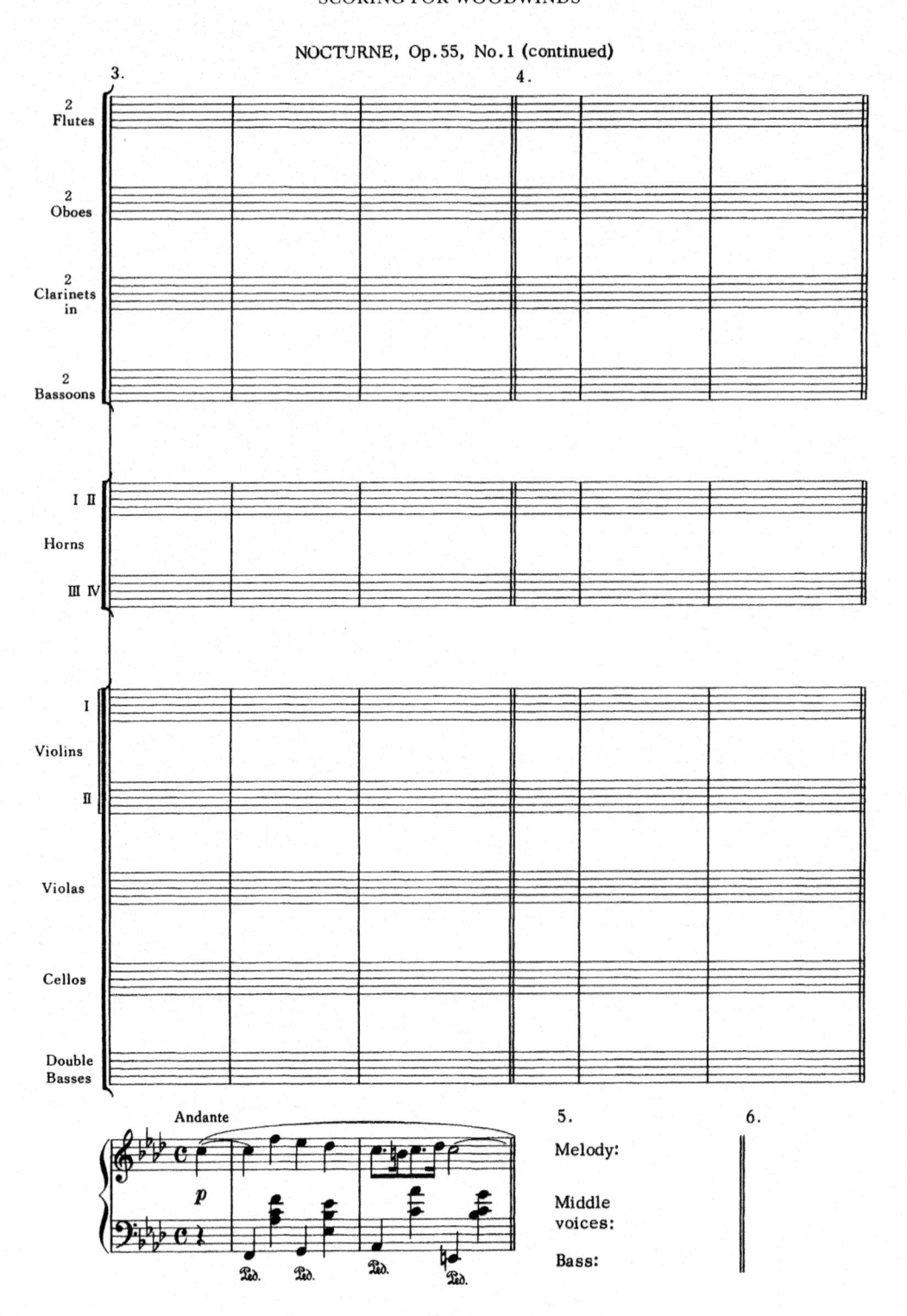

SCORING FOR WOODWINDS

NOCTURNE, Op. 55, No. 1 (continued)

5. Melody:

   Middle voices:

   Bass:

Score for woodwinds, horns (if desired), and strings. The scoring should reflect the antiphonal character of the music.

SONATA, Op. 27, No. 1 — Beethoven

Score for woodwinds in pairs, four horns, and strings.

VARIATIONS AND FUGUE ON A THEME BY HANDEL — Brahms

Score for woodwinds, horns (if desired), and strings. From measure 13 on, there are good opportunities for changing colors and antiphonal effects.

This excerpt is also suitable for an assignment in scoring for woodwinds alone or strings alone, although neither group alone is as effective as a combination of the two.

SONATINA, Op. 13, No. 1

Kabalevsky

PERCUSSION
Chapters 13, 14

1. Write a part for four timpani. For the initial tuning, try to select pitches that will fit into the harmonies throughout the piece (at the points where timpani are being used). If changes in tuning are felt to be necessary, remember to allow at least three or four measures of rest for each change and to indicate which timpano is to be changed.
2. The second blank staff may be used either for a part for one or more other percussion instruments or for another (alternative) timpani part. The instructor should specify which of these is to be done.
3. This music may also be used as the basis for an assignment in scoring for woodwinds, horns, and strings or for full orchestra.

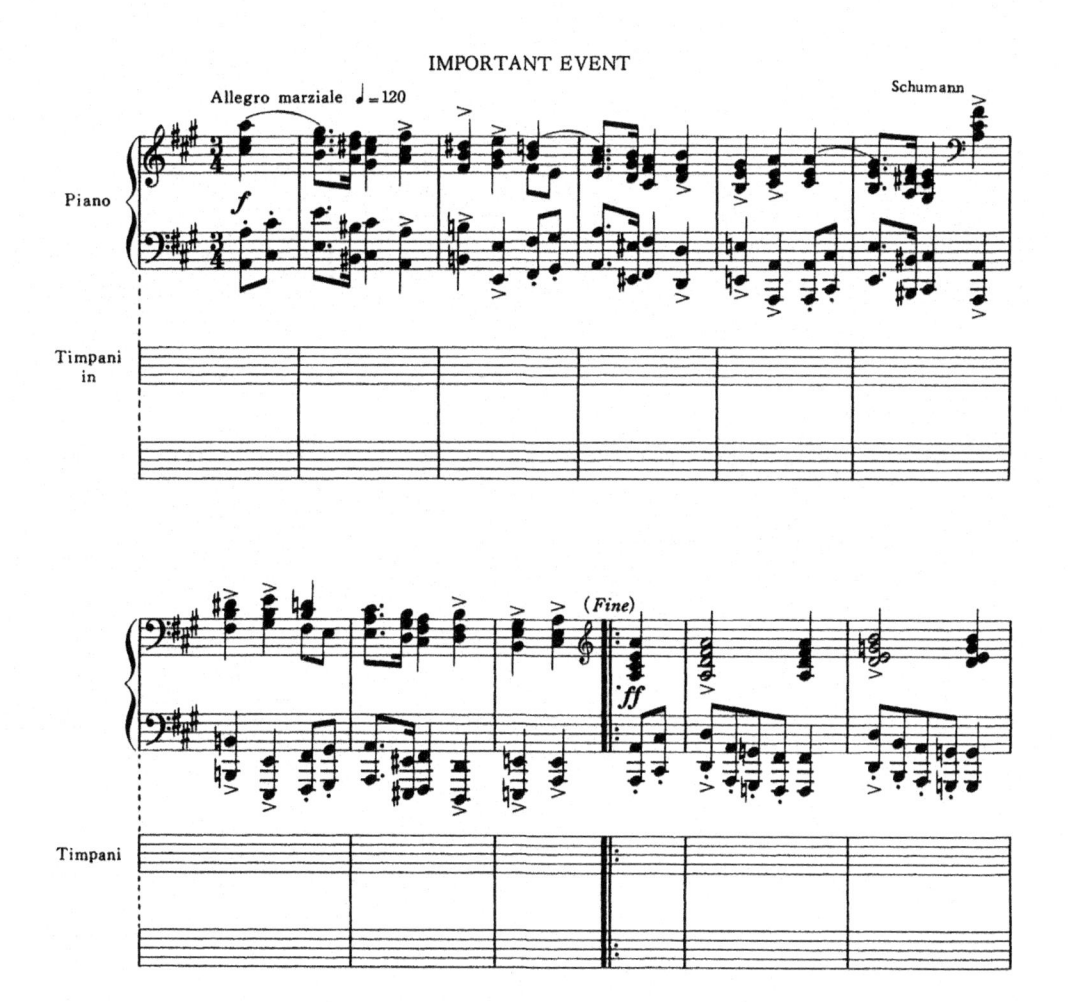

IMPORTANT EVENT

Schumann

PERCUSSION

IMPORTANT EVENT, continued

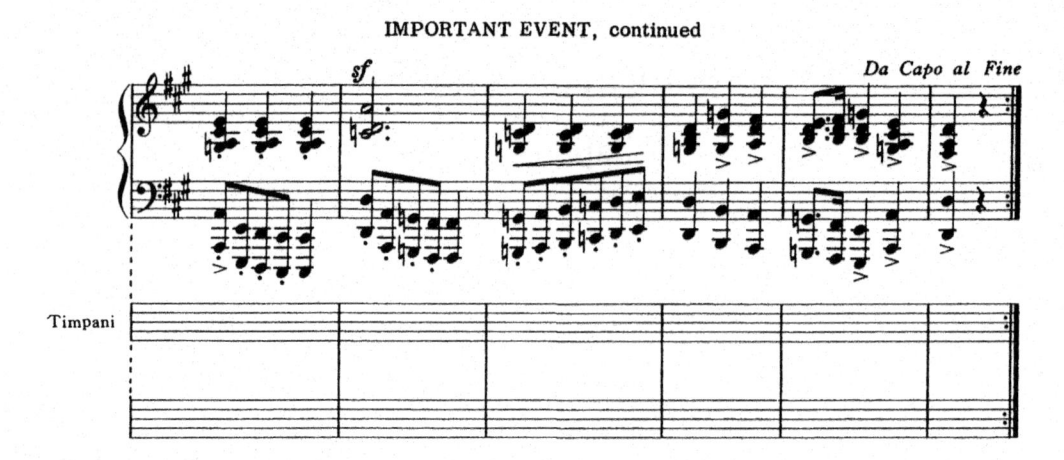

The instructor is to specify in which of the following ways the next excerpt is to be used:

a. Imagine that the music is to be scored for orchestra and write parts here for at least four percussion instruments. Except for those of definite pitch, two instruments may be written on the same staff if necessary.
b. On another sheet, actually score the music for orchestra and include parts for at least four percussion instruments.

PRELUDE 24
From 24 Preludes

PERCUSSION

The instructor is to specify in which of the following ways these excerpts are to be used:

a. Imagine that the music is to be scored for orchestra and write parts here for at least four percussion instruments. Except for those of definite pitch, two instruments may be written on the same staff if necessary.
b. On another sheet, actually score the music for orchestra and include parts for at least four percussion instruments.

MARCH
From "The Love of Three Oranges"
Prokofiev

HARP
Chapter 15

Rewriting Exercises for Harp

Rewrite the following passages for harp in such a way as to involve the fewest possible pedal changes. Do not omit notes but change spellings where that will eliminate pedal changes. Include a pedal setting at the beginning of each exercise and indicate pedal changes as they occur. Each of these exercises can be rewritten so as to require only one pedal change.

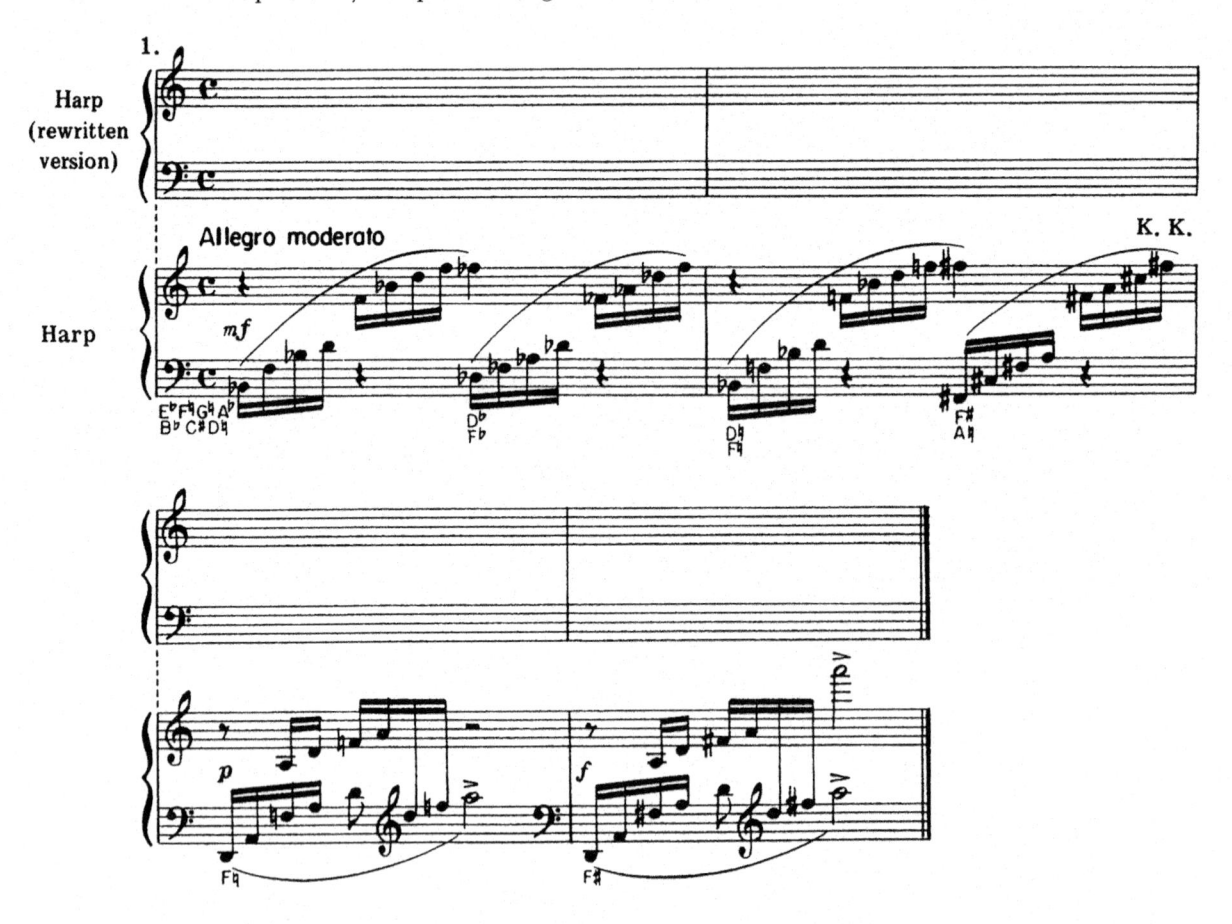

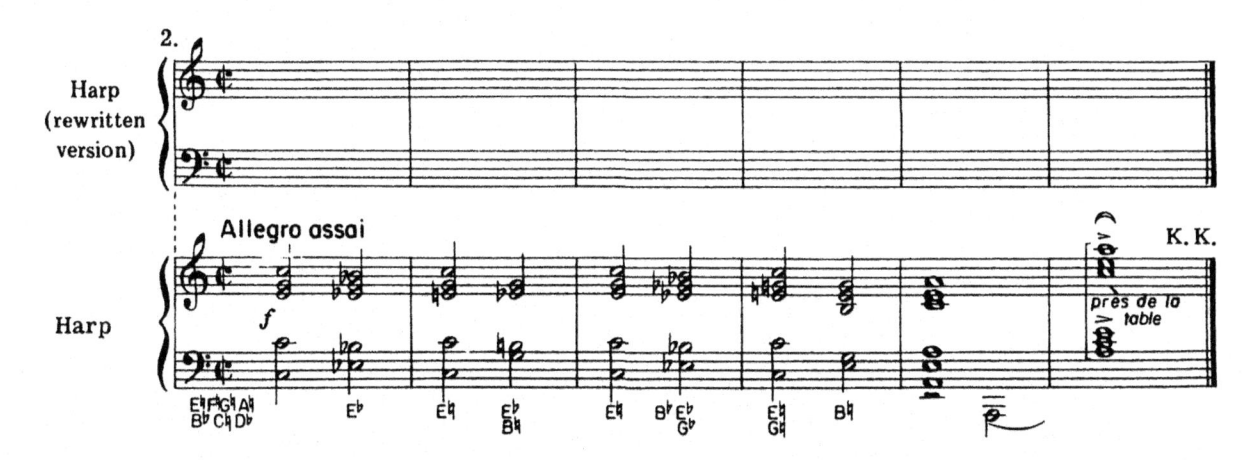

Harp Exercises

In Exercises 1 and 2, rewrite (respell) the passages in such a way as to involve the fewest possible pedal changes. Include a pedal setting at the beginning of each exercise and indicate pedal changes as they occur. These exercises can be rewritten so as to require only two and four pedal changes, respectively.

In Exercise 3, add the appropriate accidentals to the letters given below each chord to show the pedal setting that would be needed if the chord were to be played as a glissando on the harp. Also show each pedal setting in diagram form.

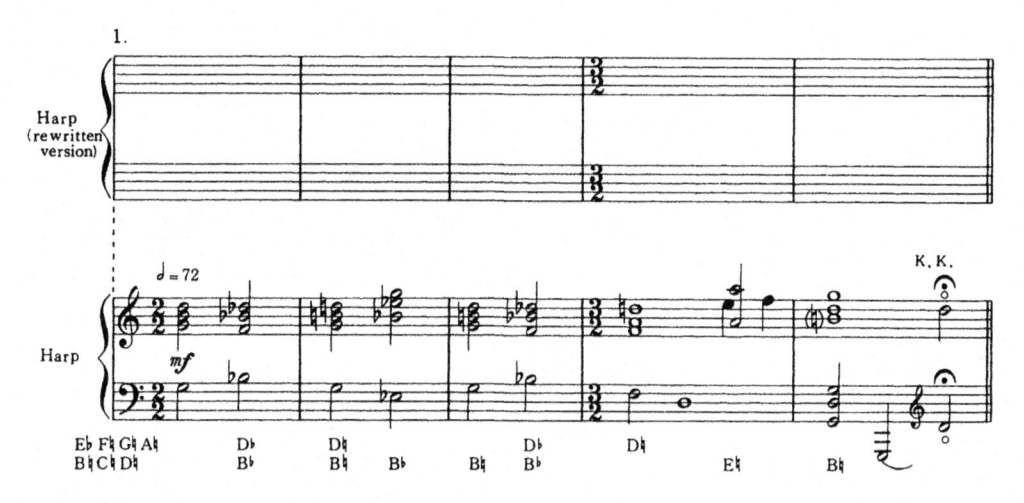

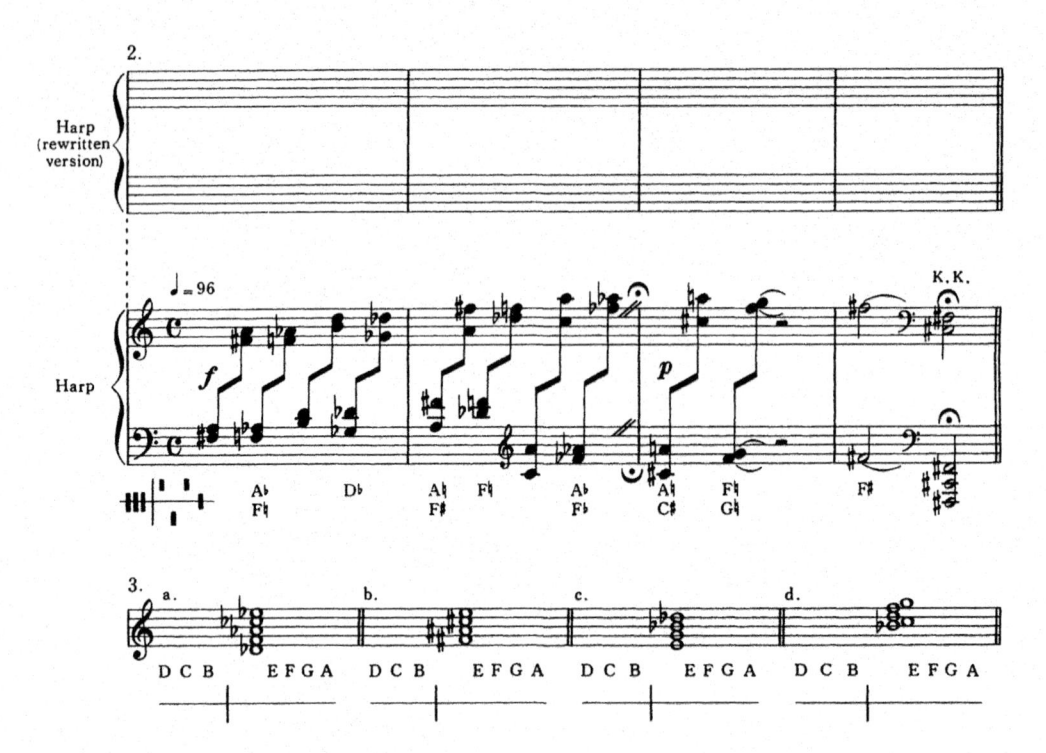

HARP

ORCHESTRA
Chapter 16

Score for woodwinds, horns, and strings, plus percussion—and harp, if desired. Meter changes must be inserted at the actual measures where they occur. This piece is also suitable for an assignment in scoring for strings alone.

NO. 12 From FIFTEEN HUNGARIAN PEASANT SONGS

Bartók

Copyright 1920 by Universal Edition; Renewed 1948. Copyright and Renewal Assigned to Boosey & Hawkes Inc. for the U.S.A. Reprinted by permission of Boosey & Hawkes Inc. ©Copyright 1920 Universal Edition. Used by permission.

Score for orchestra. Aim for maximum brilliance and fullness.

CRUSADERS' HYMN

ORCHESTRA

Exercise in Error Detection (Scoring for Orchestra)

Leaving aside questions of stylistic appropriateness, point out, on this page or on a separate sheet, errors or instances of questionable scoring in the following. Alternatively, this exercise may be done orally in class.

WACHET AUF

J. S. Bach

ORCHESTRA

Score for orchestra. Harp may be included but should not be depended upon entirely for the rolled chords; strings should also take them.

This piece is also suitable for an assignment in scoring for woodwinds, horns, and strings.

NO. 1, From Fifteen Hungarian Peasant Songs

Bartók

Copyright 1920 by Universal Edition; Renewed 1948. Copyright and Renewal Assigned to Boosey & Hawkes Inc. for the U.S.A. Reprinted by permission of Boosey & Hawkes Inc. ©Copyright 1920 Universal Edition. Used by permission.

ORCHESTRA

Score for a "Schumann" orchestra: woodwinds in pairs, four horns, two trumpets, two trombones, timpani, and strings. Use all the instruments in the first eight measures (and later if desired). The gaps in the open-spaced harmonies at the start may be filled in where that seems desirable, whereas the closely spaced chords in the left hand (measures 10, 11, etc.) should be respaced so as to be less muddy. In measure 17, consider the effect of the pedal.

FANTASIA, OP. 17

Score for orchestra.

A DESERTED FARM

MacDowell

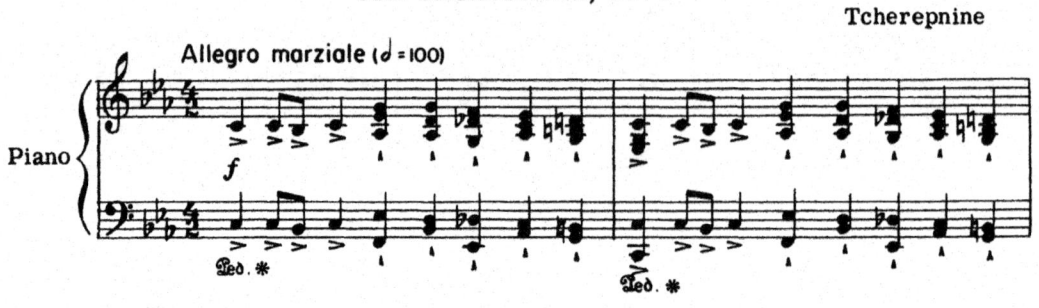

ORCHESTRA

Score for orchestra. Note particularly the differences in dynamics that are called for.

BAGATELLE No. 1
from
TEN BAGATELLES, OP. 5

Tcherepnine

BAGATELLE NO. 1 (continued)

ORCHESTRA

Score for orchestra (or only woodwinds, horns, and strings plus harp, if desired). Note the effect of the pedal indications, especially in the closing measures of the excerpt.

NOTTURNO

GRIEG

15
p a tempo.
poco
Ped.
18
p
poco
Ped.
21 Più mosso.
pp
Ped. una corda
Ped.
21
ppp
poco a poco
cresc.
Ped.
24
Ped. tre corde
molto
ff
Ped.
27
poco rit.
etc.

ORCHESTRA

Score for an orchestra consisting of woodwinds in pairs, two horns, two trumpets, three trombones, two timpani, and strings.

SONATA, OP. 143

Schubert

ORCHESTRA

Score for voice and an orchestra consisting of one flute, one oboe, one B♭ clarinet, one bassoon, one horn, one trumpet (C), one trombone, harp, and a string section of about ten, eight, six, four, two (the instrumentation used by the composer in scoring this work). If possible, the instructor should obtain the score (*Eight Poems of Emily Dickinson*) so that students may compare their completed scores with Copland's.

To Marcelle de Manziarly

5. Heart, we will forget him

Music by
AARON COPLAND

*Grace note on the beat

© Copyright 1951 by The Aaron Copland Fund for Music, Inc., Copyright Renewed. Used by permission of Boosey & Hawkes, Inc., Sole Agent.

moving forward
When you have done, pray tell me,
Ped. sim.
faster
rit. e dim. (gradual
That I my thoughts may dim
molto marc.
return to a tempo)
Haste lest while you're lag - ging, I
may re - mem - ber him.
Ped.

Exercises in Scoring in the Styles of Debussy and Strauss

These fragments attempt to imitate the musical styles of Debussy and Strauss, respectively, and were written expressly to serve as exercises in orchestrating in the manner of these composers. That is, Exercise 1 is to be scored as Debussy might have scored it, Exercise 2 as Strauss might have scored it. This assignment obviously assumes a previous study of orchestral works of these composers.

Octave doublings may be used wherever they seem appropriate. The instrumentation chosen in each case should be typical of that employed by the composer whose style is being imitated.

ORCHESTRA

Score for orchestra. Analyze first, marking appearances of the subject (or answer). Although no dynamics are included in the original, they must be supplied in the score. This fugue is most often played at a tempo of about ♩ = 58–60.

FUGUE VII
(WELL TEMPERED CLAVIER, Volume II)

J.S. Bach

ORCHESTRA

Score for orchestra.

ORCHESTRA

Score for orchestra. Because of the many departures from the key signature in this composition, it will probably prove easiest to write the orchestral score without a key signature, accidentals being inserted instead. Compare your completed scoring with the published orchestral version.

This music is also suitable for an assignment in scoring for woodwinds, horns, and strings (plus harp, celesta, or any other instruments desired).

ORCHESTRA

THE WHITE PEACOCK, continued

ORCHESTRA

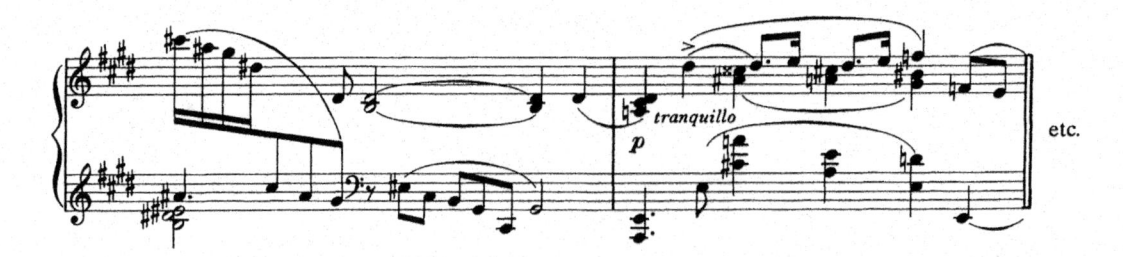

Score for orchestra. The first half of this piece, orchestrated by the composer, is given in Chapter 11 of the textbook. Compare your completed scoring with that.

This piece is also suitable for an assignment in scoring for: (1) woodwinds plus extra woodwinds and/or horns; (2) woodwinds, horns, and strings.

BAGATELLE 8. From Twelve Bagatelles

George Rochberg

Copyright 1955, by Theodore Presser Co. Used by permission.

Score for orchestra. Make some use of special color effects (percussion, harp or piano, etc.).

MARCH, OP. 12, No. 1

Allegro ma non troppo

Prokofiev

ORCHESTRA

Some 32 measures, involving the repetition of themes already stated, are omitted here. The closing measures of the piece follow.

SCORING FOR HIGH SCHOOL ORCHESTRA
Chapter 19

Score for high school orchestra, transposing the piece to another key to avoid the six-flat key signature in the second section and to allow for more resonance and easier fingering in the strings throughout. Include cues where that seems advisable (see Chapter 19 of the textbook). Or, score a symphony orchestra, retaining the original key if desired.

GOLLIWOGG'S CAKE WALK
from
"The Children's Corner"

Debussy

SCORING FOR HIGH SCHOOL ORCHESTRA

From CHILDREN'S CORNER. Copyright 1908 Durand S.A. Used By Permission Of The Publisher, Theodore Presser Company, Sole Representative U.S.A.